GUILTY
BY A HAIR!

Real-life DNA Matches!

Anna Prokos

WARNING: In this book, investigators look for **DNA** in some disgusting places. They can find it in bloodstains. They get it from chewed-up food and pulled-out hair. There is also plenty of **DNA** in dead bodies. So . . . read at your own risk.

Franklin Watts®
A Division of Scholastic Inc.
New York • Toronto • London • Auckland • Sydney
Mexico City • New Delhi • Hong Kong
Danbury, Connecticut

CONTENTS

FORENSIC 411

Get the 411 on DNA, and find out how investigators use it to solve crimes.

8 OVERHEARD IN THE LAB
Discussing DNA

10 SEE FOR YOURSELF
A Drop of Evidence

12 WHO'S WHO?
The Forensic Team

These stories are 100% real. Find out how investigators have used DNA to solve mysteries that seemed 100% impossible.

DNA on a burger solves a crime in Suffolk, VA.

15 Case #1:
The Case of the Hungry Burglars
Three men eat a hamburger just before they rob a fast-food restaurant. Will the burger bite them back?

Case #2:
A Hair of Evidence
A woman disappears. Can a few cat hairs help solve the mystery?

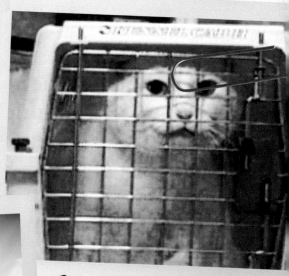

Cat hair holds the key to a murder in Canada.

35 Case #3:
A Second Look at the Evidence
A man goes to jail for shooting a policeman. But did the police get the right man?

Will DNA evidence free a prisoner in Boston, MA?

FORENSIC DOWNLOAD

DNA is in almost every cell of your body. And information about it is on every page of this section.

44 FLASHBACK
Key Dates in the Study of DNA

RIPPED FROM
THE HEADLINES **46**
In the News

48 REAL STUFF
It's All Genetic

52 CAREERS
**Help Wanted:
DNA Scientist**

YELLOW PAGES

56 RESOURCES

59 DICTIONARY

62 INDEX

64 AUTHOR'S NOTE

All it would take is one sneeze. Your **DNA** would be all over this book. That's right. Your spit has **DNA** in it.

FORENSIC 411

That's important to police because everyone's **DNA** is different. With the right equipment, detectives can match a person with his spit. They've put criminals in jail that way. They've also freed innocent people.

IN THIS SECTION:

- ▶ how DNA experts TALK;
- ▶ where INVESTIGATORS look for DNA evidence;
- ▶ who else works at the CRIME SCENES.

Discussing DNA

Forensic DNA specialists have their own way of talking. Find out what their vocabulary means.

"We didn't find any fingerprints. But let's take that soda can and the T-shirt. We can check for **DNA** evidence back at the lab."

DNA
(DEE-en-ay) a chemical found in almost every cell of your body. It's a blueprint for the way you look and function. No two people have the same DNA (except identical twins).

DNA profiling
(DEE-en-ay PROH-fyl-ing) a way of processing DNA samples so they can be compared with other samples. The DNA comes from samples of saliva, blood, urine, and other bodily fluids or tissues.

DNA stands for Deoxyribonucleic Acid.

"We need **DNA profiling** done on this guy. Who has his sample?"

"I'd say that we are looking for a thief with a specific **trait**: white-blond hair that's really straight."

trait
(trayt) a specific feature of something. For example, your hair color is one of your traits.

"Look, I know this criminal seems like a real monster, but he's got 46 **chromosomes** in his cells—same as you and me."

chromosomes
(KROH-muh-sohms) thread-like structures in the center of a cell. They're made of DNA and contain all the genetic information in your body.

"Most people in my family are redheads. I guess it's just in my **genes**."

genes
(jeens) tiny pieces of DNA. Genes determine general stuff, like the fact that you have two eyes, a nose, and a mouth. They also determine specific stuff, like the color of your eyes, hair, and skin.

Say What?

Here's some other lingo a **DNA specialist** might use on the job.

bag
(bag) take as evidence
*"**Bag** that piece of gum. It might have the perp's DNA."*

degrade
(dee-GRADE) to break down into small unusable parts
*"Don't leave those DNA samples out in the hot police car. They'll **degrade**, and then they'll be worthless."*

perp
(purp) a person who has committed a crime. It's short for *perpetrator.*
*"It always feels good to send a **perp** to jail."*

swab
(swahb) to use a thick, cotton tip on a stick—like a Q-tip, only bigger—to get samples of DNA from suspects
*"**Swab** the inside of the suspect's cheek before you question him."*

Fast Facts

DNA is the world's smallest instruction manual.

▶ There's a copy of your DNA in almost every cell in your body. That means that every cell has a complete set of instructions for making another you!

▶ If you compared two people's DNA, you'd see that they're 99.9% the same. Only 0.1% is different. That the part that makes you, you! And that's the part that scientists use to identify a person.

▶ Under the right conditions, DNA can survive a long time! DNA has been found in Egyptian mummies!

A Drop of Evidence

Spit. Blood. Skin. DNA evidence lives in almost every cell of your body.

Think of DNA as your chemical **signature**. No one else's is quite like yours. That makes DNA a great way to identify people.

What's more, almost every cell in your body contains DNA. Almost everywhere you go, you leave a trail of chemical fingerprints. That fact has put many a criminal in jail —and the police know it.

Detectives search crime scenes for **evidence** that might contain DNA. There's DNA in skin, hair, blood, saliva, sweat, and other body fluids. So they look for anything a perp might have touched, licked, bled on, sweated in, or sneezed on. In the bathroom, DNA could be on the handle of a toilet flusher—or in the toilet itself!

Take a look at the photos on this page. These are just some of the places that might hide traces of DNA. They might look like ordinary household items. But any one of them could hold the key to putting a criminal behind bars.

11

The Forensic Team

DNA specialists work as part of a team to help solve crimes and identify victims.

FORENSIC DNA ANALYSTS
They examine, analyze, and interpret DNA samples in the lab. They determine if these samples could have been left by victims or suspects.

MEDICAL EXAMINERS
They're medical doctors who investigate suspicious deaths. They try to find out when and how someone died.

DETECTIVES OR AGENTS
They direct the crime investigation. They collect information about the crime and interview witnesses. They identify suspects—and arrest them if there's enough evidence!

TRACE EVIDENCE SPECIALISTS
They collect trace evidence at the scene. That includes fibers, tire tracks, shoe prints, and more.

FORENSIC ANTHROPOLOGISTS
They're called in to identify victims by studying bones.

FINGERPRINT SPECIALISTS
They find, photograph, and collect fingerprints at the scene. Then they compare them to prints they have on record.

TRUE-LIFE CASE FILES!

24 hours a day, 7 days a week, 365 days a year, DNA specialists are solving mysteries.

IN THIS SECTION:

- ▶ how a HALF-EATEN HAMBURGER helped catch a thief;
- ▶ why police RELIED ON A CAT to find a murderer;
- ▶ how DNA helped FREE AN INNOCENT MAN.

Here's how forensic DNA specialists get the job done.

What does it take to solve a crime? Good DNA specialists don't just make guesses. They're scientists. They follow a step-by-step process.

As you read the case studies, you can follow along with them. Keep an eye out for the icons below. They'll clue you in to each step along the way.

THE QUESTION At the beginning of each case, the DNA specialists have to identify **one or two main questions** they have to answer.

THE EVIDENCE The specialists' next step is to **gather and analyze evidence**. Specialists gather as much information as they can. Then they study it and figure out what it means.

THE CONCLUSION Along the way, the specialists come up with theories about what may have happened. They test these theories against the evidence. Does the evidence back up the theory? **If so, they've reached a conclusion.**

The Case of the Hungry Burglars

Suffolk, Virginia
May 2, 2004

Three men eat a hamburger just before they rob a fast-food restaurant. Will the burger bite them back?

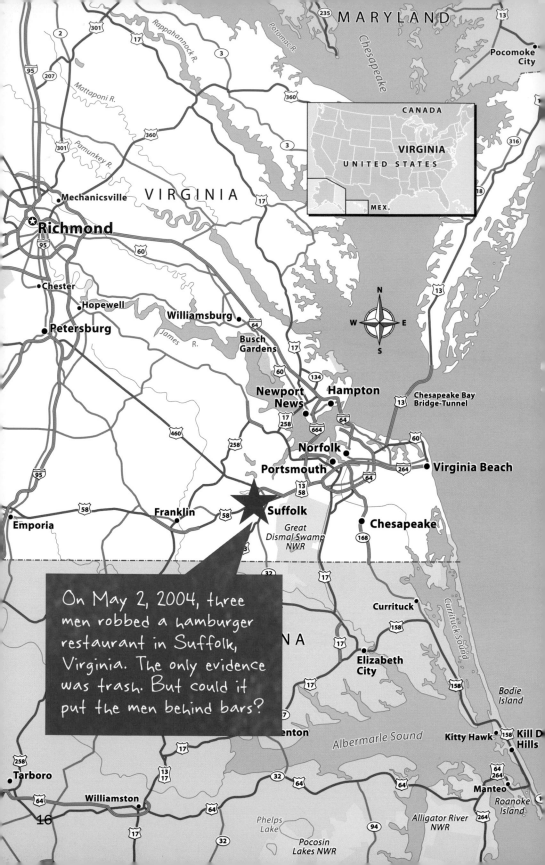

MARYLAND

Pocomoke
City

Chesapeake

CANADA

VIRGINIA
UNITED STATES

MEX.

VIRGINIA

Rappahannock R.

Potomac R.

Mattaponi R.

Pamunkey R.

Mechanicsville

Richmond

Chester

Hopewell

Williamsburg

Busch
Gardens

James R.

Petersburg

Newport
News

Hampton

Chesapeake Bay
Bridge-Tunnel

Norfolk

Virginia Beach

Portsmouth

Suffolk

Chesapeake

Franklin

Great
Dismal Swamp
NWR

Emporia

On May 2, 2004, three
men robbed a hamburger
restaurant in Suffolk,
Virginia. The only evidence
was trash. But could it
put the men behind bars?

Currituck

Elizabeth
City

Currituck Sound

Bodie
Island

enton

Albermarle Sound

Kitty Hawk

Kill D
Hills

Tarboro

Williamston

Manteo

Roanoke
Island

Phelps
Lake

Pocosin
Lakes NWR

Alligator River
NWR

Burger Bandits

**The burglars escaped with cash from the restaurant.
Did they leave any clues?**

It was just before closing time at a fast-food restaurant in Suffolk, Virginia. Three hungry men ordered their food and sat down to eat. They shared two burgers, fries, and one drink. They ate most of their food.

The three men waited until five minutes before closing time. They stood up, threw their trash away, and robbed the restaurant at gunpoint.

The burglars demanded money. They forced the scared workers into the restaurant freezer. They then ran out the door. A witness outside the restaurant saw the men sprinting away—and called the police.

The robbers shared a burger and fries before they robbed the restaurant. Could the remains of that meal provide the police with evidence?

Within minutes, officers arrived at the scene. They searched the area for the robbers. But they had disappeared.

The police went inside and started searching the crime scene. They made an important discovery. All the trash had been taken out just before the robbery. That meant that the only garbage in the restaurant came from the robbers. It could be important evidence. Police radioed for help. This was a job for a DNA **specialist**.

Bag It

A forensic technician collected the evidence. Then she had to keep it from spoiling.

Suffolk County's Forensic Unit supervisor, Joan Jones, got the call at 11:30 P.M. When she arrived at the scene, she was briefed about the situation. The officers told her about the garbage bags.

Did the burglars leave traces of DNA behind on their food? It was Jones's job to find out.

She quickly slipped on her latex gloves and dug in. Jones recovered a half-eaten burger, a tiny portion of another burger, a pack of fries, and a drink with a straw.

Normally, Jones seals evidence in a paper bag. Paper bags keep most things safe from light and **contamination**. But in this case, paper wasn't enough. The food might spoil before it got to the lab. Saliva from the burger, fries, or straw could seep into the paper. It was too big a risk. So Jones collected the evidence in a plastic bag and sealed it. Then she drove it to her office and put it in the freezer.

Jones filled out the paperwork. She signed the **chain-of-custody form**, showing who had handled the evidence. The next morning, she drove the frozen food to the Virginia Department of Forensic Science for analysis.

Joan Jones is the supervisor of the Suffolk County Forensic Unit. She carefully collected the evidence from the fast-food restaurant.

Jones examined the remains of a meal like this one.

BAG IT CAREFULLY!

Investigators have to keep a close eye on DNA evidence.

To crime scene investigators, DNA evidence is gold. The right evidence can lock up a murderer or free an innocent man.

Handle with Care

To protect their cases, investigators handle DNA with care. They keep samples out of humidity, direct sunlight, and rain.

These conditions degrade DNA and make it useless. Handlers use gloves so they don't mix their own DNA with the samples. They wear masks so they don't breathe, spit, or sneeze on the evidence.

Chain-of-Custody

Investigators also keep detailed reports to show who handles the evidence. Everyone who touches the evidence signs a chain-of-custody form. At the crime scene, officers make notes about when and where evidence is found. The evidence then gets stored in a safe place.

Only certain people are allowed to handle it. Anyone who examines or tests the evidence adds notes to the chain-of-custody.

The chain-of-custody records can be used in court. They help prove that no one has messed up the evidence.

Put to the Test

**The crime lab had four pieces of evidence to work.
Could they recover DNA from a half-eaten burger?**

At the lab, the bag of frozen food made its way to Ann Pollard. Pollard is a **forensic** scientist trained to work with DNA evidence.

The food had just been tested for fingerprints. The investigator found prints on the paper wrappers, the fry box, and the cup lids. But he couldn't match the prints with a **suspect**.

Ann Pollard, a DNA scientist for the Virginia Department of Forensic Science. She ran lab tests of DNA she found on the burglars' burgers and fries.

It was Pollard's turn to look at the evidence. Her first task was to get saliva samples from the food. She took a cotton swab and poked around the bitten areas of the burger. The cup and the straw had already been swabbed.

Next, Pollard used a **scalpel** to remove the swabs from their long sticks. She put the swabs in a tube and added chemicals. Then she heated the sample. The chemicals remove everything from the swab except DNA. The heat speeds up the removal process. After half an hour, Pollard had **isolated** the DNA. Now, she was ready to test it.

Pollard put the sample into the lab's workstation. This high-tech equipment processes the DNA so it can be x-rayed.

Pollard needed to be sure she had enough

21

Cotton swabs are sometimes used to collect DNA information. The evidence is then stored in tubes like this one. Ann Pollard used swabs on the bitten areas of the burger found at the crime scene.

information to work with. So, she moved the sample to a thermocycler. The thermocycler used a process called **polymerase chain reaction** (PCR) to make millions of copies of the DNA.

Finally, Pollard was ready to make an image of the DNA. She used a machine called a FMBIO. The result was a familiar sight: the DNA bar code.

After a month of testing, Pollard finally had the results in her hand. The samples produced three separate DNA profiles. Each of the burglars had left his mark on the tiny scraps of food.

The challenge now was to find out whom the DNA profiles belonged to.

This film shows a DNA profile that can be compared and studied.

Happy Meal Match-Up

The testing found three DNA profiles. The robbers shared a meal; now they would share the punishment.

Pollard went to a computer and logged into the state's **CODIS**. CODIS stands for Combined DNA Index System. CODIS is a giant file of DNA profiles. When police charge a suspect with a crime, they take DNA samples. They enter the information into a computer system. Most states have their own CODIS. So does the **FBI**.

For more information about CODIS, go to page 24.

Pollard entered her three DNA profiles into the system. The computer tried to match them with profiles already on file. Eventually, she had her answer. CODIS came up with matches.

Suffolk County police now had their suspects. But they still had to check the CODIS results. An officer visited the men. She collected their DNA by swabbing the inside of their cheeks. The sample was analyzed to produce a DNA profile. CODIS was right. The DNA matched the samples from the fast-food leftovers.

Using CODIS allows police to match DNA samples with suspects.

All three suspects confessed to the crime. Police got the burglars off the streets—thanks to some high-tech science and a little chewed-up food. **24/7**

THE BIG BRAIN

CODIS is a computer database packed with DNA samples.

Say you're a police investigator. You go to a crime scene and find some evidence. You take it back to the lab. The DNA **experts** tell you you've got a great sample of someone's DNA.

They just don't know *who* that someone is. You've still got to find a suspect.

Wouldn't it be great if there were an easier way?

DNA Database

In fact there is. The FBI has created a DNA database. It's called CODIS. That stands for Combined DNA Index System.

CODIS contains DNA samples of more than 300,000 convicted people. Some states enter only convicted criminals. Other states enter people when they are arrested.

Who's in CODIS?

These days, laws in all 50 states support CODIS. Anyone convicted of a sex offense or murder must have his or her DNA entered into the system.

Sure, investigators still have to look for perps. But CODIS sometimes gives them a break.

In this case, a half-eaten burger led police to some burglars. Can a few hairs help investigators find a murderer?

A Hair of Evidence

**A woman disappears. Can a
few cat hairs help solve
the mystery?**

Missing Without a Trace

People don't just disappear. Or do they?

Shirley Duguay at her home on Prince Edward Island, in Canada. Soon after this photo was taken, she disappeared.

It was the morning of October 3, 1994. Off the east coast of Canada, winter was coming to Prince Edward Island. The ground was dotted with fallen leaves. A chill hung in the air. Cold waves pounded the base of the island's huge cliffs.

Shirley Duguay left home that day— and didn't return. She was 32. She cared for five children as a single mom. When friends realized she was missing, they figured she was visiting relatives. But when they called the relatives, Duguay wasn't there.

Relatives soon arrived at Duguay's house. They decided not to call the police. Duguay's ex-husband, Douglas Beamish, lived nearby with his parents. He was known to have a bad temper. Duguay's relatives were afraid he might get the children. Or they could be sent to foster care.

Besides, they felt certain that Shirley Duguay would walk in the door any minute. She never did.

Iles de
la Madeleine

CANADA
**PRINCE EDWARD
ISLAND**

UNITED STATES

MEX.

North Cape

Miminegash

Alberton

O'Leary

PRINCE EDWARD ISLAND

Egmont
Bay

Malpeque
Bay

North
Bustico

Prince Edward
Island NP

North
Lake

St. Peters

Summerside

Mount
Stewart

Cardigan

Borden-
Carleton

Charlottetown

Orwell

NEW
BRUNSWICK

Cape
Tormentine

Northumberland Strait

Murray
Harbour

Wood
Islands

Amherst

Oxford

In the fall of 1994, a woman
from Prince Edward Island, Canada,
seemed to disappear into thin air.
It turned out that the main clue
to her disappearance was invisible
to the naked eye.

Minas Basin

Maitland

NOVA SCOTIA

Wolfville

Shubenacadie

Windsor

Sheet
Harbour

New Ross

Dartmouth

Halifax

ATLANTIC OCEAN

Strange Clues

The police found Shirley Duguay's car. But where was she?

Four days after Shirley Duguay disappeared, police found her car. It was empty, but there were bloodstains on the windows. Clearly, someone had been hurt—maybe even killed.

Police traced the car to Duguay. They questioned her family. Her relatives admitted that they hadn't seen her in four days.

The police launched a massive search. Hundreds of people joined in.

Three weeks later, a clue turned up. Fifteen miles (24 km) from Duguay's car, police discovered a man's leather jacket and running shoes stuffed in a plastic bag. The jacket was covered with blood.

The police examined the jacket carefully. They tested the blood on the jacket. It was the same blood type as Duguay. They also found short, white hairs stuck to the jacket. But there was still no sign of Duguay.

Soon, the island was covered in snow. Police

Members of Canada's top police force, the Royal Canadian Mounted Police, arrived in Prince Edward Island to search for Shirley Duguay.

The police built a tent over the spot that Shirley Duguay's body was found.

were forced to give up the search. All winter, Duguay's disappearance remained a mystery.

Then, the following May, a fisherman found Shirley Duguay's body in the woods. She was dead, and it was clear that she had been murdered.

WHAT'S YOUR TYPE?

All blood looks alike. But it's not.

Blood comes in different types. There are two things that determine your blood type. First, each person's blood is Type A, B, AB, or O. Second, your blood can be RH+ or RH-, depending on whether or not it has stuff in it called the **RH factor**.

If you lose a lot of blood, you'll need more. But you can't get blood from just anyone. The donor must have the right blood type.

If Your Blood Type Is	You Can Get Blood From
A+	A+, A-, O+, O-
A-	A-, O-
B+	B+, B-, O+, O-
B-	B-, O-
AB+	anyone
AB-	AB-, A-, B-, O-
O+	O+, O-
O-	O-

O- is the universal donor. Anyone can use it.
AB+ is the universal receiver. An AB+ can get blood from anyone.

29

Snowball's Chance

The police couldn't crack the case. Could a cat possibly help?

Police now knew they had a murder case on their hands. They also had a suspect: Duguay's ex-husband, Douglas Beamish.

Detectives looked into Beamish's background. They didn't like what they found. Beamish had a history of violence.

Police questioned Beamish. He had an **alibi** for the day Duguay disappeared. He told police he had been working on a house he was building. But witnesses had spotted his car near Duguay's house. Other people saw cuts on his hands that day.

"His story just didn't add up," says Inspector Alphonse MacNeil, who was in charge of the investigation.

But MacNeil couldn't prove a thing. Beamish denied he was involved in Duguay's murder. And no one had seen it happen.

The police had to rely on the physical evidence. They went back to the clue the killer left behind—the jacket. Beamish had owned a jacket like it. And there was blood on it that was the same type as Duguay's. But that wasn't enough evidence. How could they link Beamish to the jacket?

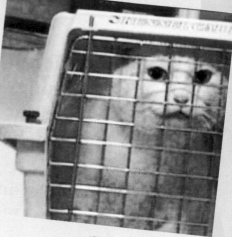

This cat, Snowball, belonged to Douglas Beamish's parents. Had those white hairs on the leather jacket come from this cat?

One of the detectives, Roger Savoie, remembered the white hairs on the jacket. He also remembered that Beamish's parents had a white cat named Snowball.

Could it be that the hairs belonged to Snowball? If they did, a **jury** might believe that Beamish killed Shirley.

THE QUESTION

A Purrfect Match?

Sometimes scientists are the best detectives.

How could the police prove that the hairs came from Snowball? To the naked eye, all white cat hair looks alike. Even a microscope wouldn't yield an answer. Proof would have to come from Snowball's DNA.

The idea was new to everyone involved. Animal DNA had never been used in court. Could it be done? And would a judge allow **prosecutors** to use the evidence?

Investigators decided to take a chance.

The police took a sample of Snowball's blood and stored it in a container like this one. **THE EVIDENCE** The DNA in Snowball's blood was compared to the DNA in the cat hair.

They used the Internet to search for an expert in cat genetics. They found what they were looking for at a lab in Maryland.

The police took a sample of Snowball's blood. They sent it to Stephen O'Brien, director of the lab. Included in the package were the white hairs from the jacket.

26 ISO 64

26 26A

At the lab, scientists began the complicated process of creating a DNA profile. First, they separated the DNA from cells in the hair and the blood. Then they added chemicals to each sample to process the DNA. Finally, they took an x-ray of each sample. The end result was a set of images. Each image looked like a profile for the blood and for the hair.

O'Brien had one result for the hair from the jacket and one for Snowball's blood. He compared the two results. They matched.

THE CONCLUSION Detective Savoie's hunch was right. The hair from the jacket contained the same DNA as the blood from Snowball.

Case Closed

Would the jury think Beamish was guilty?

The police arrested Douglas Beamish for murder. During the trial, prosecutors questioned Beamish's brother. He told the jury about a letter Beamish sent to Duguay. There was "no point in living" if he and Duguay couldn't be together, Beamish had written. Then he signed the letter in blood! Prosecutors argued that Beamish killed Duguay because she had decided to end their marriage.

Next, the prosecutors presented the physical evidence. They showed the jacket they had found in the woods. It was identical to one Beamish owned, they told the jury.

But the most damaging evidence came from Snowball. Dr. O'Brien said that the cat hairs found on the bloody jacket were Snowball's. The scientist explained to the jury how the DNA match had been made. In his opinion, Snowball and the cat hair had the same DNA profile.

Finally, it was time for the jury to decide the case. After 12 hours, they reached a **verdict**. On July 19, 1996, they found

Douglas Beamish guilty of murder. He was sentenced to 18 years in jail.

Snowball had made history! The Shirley Duguay case was the first time DNA from an animal had been used to solve a murder. In fact, Snowball's hair had been "the most **significant** piece of evidence against Beamish," said Inspector MacNeil. You might say that a cat had caught a killer. **24/7**

Douglas Beamish *(left)* and his lawyer leave the courtroom. Beamish will spend 18 years in jail for the murder of Shirley Duguay.

In this case a few cat hairs helped catch a murderer. But DNA has also helped free innocent people. Read the next case and find out how.

A Second Look at the Evidence

A man goes to jail for shooting a policeman. But did the police get the right man?

Roxbury, Massachusetts
May 30, 1997

Jailed!

Stephan Cowans was convicted of attempted murder. Had the police found the right man?

In July 1998, Stephan Cowans sat in a Boston courtroom. The prosecutor called witness after witness. Each one told the jury a piece of the story. Cowans, they said, had shot a policeman. If the jury believed them, Cowans could go to jail for 50 years.

On May 30, 1997, Sergeant Gregory Gallagher was on patrol in Roxbury, Massachusetts. In the backyard of a house, a man jumped him. They wrestled, and the attacker grabbed the policeman's gun. He shot Gallagher twice in the back. He also shot at an **eyewitness** who was watching from a nearby window.

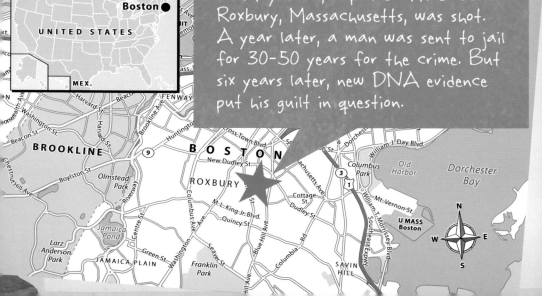

In May 1997, a police officer in Roxbury, Massachusetts, was shot. A year later, a man was sent to jail for 30–50 years for the crime. But six years later, new DNA evidence put his guilt in question.

Fingerprints usually show up well on smooth surfaces like glass. Gallagher's attacker drank from a glass just after the shooting. Investigators dusted it for prints and found a fingerprint.

The attacker ran from the scene, leaving only a baseball cap behind. He broke into a nearby home. For a minute, he held the residents **hostage**. He demanded a drink of water. He took off his sweatshirt and put down the gun. After he drank his water, he left the home and disappeared.

Two weeks later, Gallager identified Cowans from a set of eight photographs. Police arrested Cowans. They thought they had enough evidence to charge him with attempted murder. Both Gallagher and the witness from the window picked Cowans out of a **lineup**. The final piece of evidence was a fingerprint. Police found it on the water glass used by the attacker. Experts claimed that the print matched Cowans's left thumb.

In court, the evidence seemed strong. On July 6, a jury found Cowans guilty. He was sentenced to 35-50 years in jail.

Like many convicted criminals, Cowans insisted he was innocent. Could it be he was telling the truth?

Holes in the Case

The case against Cowans had some holes in it.
Could DNA evidence break it wide open?

From inside his jail cell, Cowans was determined to prove his innocence. He got in touch with the Innocence Project. Lawyers at the project work with prisoners who claim they are innocent. Eventually, Cowans's case landed on the desk of Robert N. Feldman from the New England Innocence Project.

Feldman's team of lawyers looked at his case. They found several holes. First, not all witnesses identified Cowans as the attacker. The people in the house Cowans entered got the best look at him. They failed to pick him out of a lineup.

Second, the items left behind at the crime scene were never tested. Police relied on two eyewitnesses and a single fingerprint. Eyewitnesses often make mistakes, especially when identifying people who are

The founders of the Innocence Project are Barry Scheck (*left*) and Peter Neufeld.

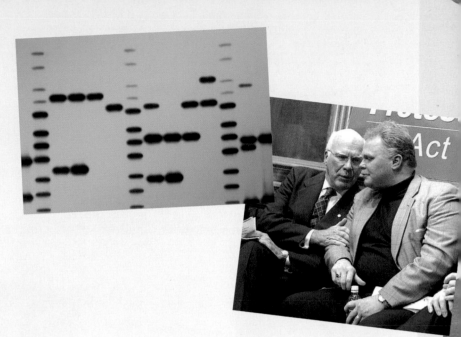

racially different than themselves. Cowans is black. Gallagher and the man in the window were white. The fingerprint, too, may have been unreliable. It was only a partial print.

Feldman and his staff decided to take the case.

The lawyers had two questions to answer. Did the attacker leave any DNA evidence at the scene? If so, did it match Cowans?

Feldman got the court to release the evidence from the case. He asked for the glass mug, the fingerprint, the sweatshirt, the gun, and the baseball cap. The team sent the items to a lab where forensic scientists got to work.

Kirk Bloodsworth *(right)*, the first person freed by the Innocence Project, sits with Senator Patrick Leahy from Vermont. *Above:* A printout from some DNA samples.

SAVED IN THE NICK OF TIME

The Innocence Project uses **DNA** evidence to free innocent prisoners.

Sometimes, people go to jail for crimes they didn't commit. That's why Barry Scheck and Peter Neufeld formed the Innocence Project in 1992. Police had just started using DNA evidence to convict criminals. Scheck and Neufeld wanted to use DNA to free innocent people.

The Innocence Project has helped to clear the names of more than 180 people who served time for crimes they didn't commit. Here's a look at just four of them.

name: David Shepard
convicted: 1984
charge: rape, robbery, weapons violations, terrorist threats
release: 1994
time served: 10 years
▶

name: Kirk Bloodsworth
convicted: 1985
charge: murder, rape
release: 1993 (first person released due to DNA evidence)
time served: 8 years

name: Brandon Moon
convicted: 1987
charge: sexual assault
release: 2004
time served: 17 years
▼

name: Gene Bibbins ▲
convicted: 1987
charge: rape, robbery
release: 2003
time served: 16 years

No Match

The defense found DNA on the hat and the glass. Did they belong to Cowans?

The court didn't release the evidence immediately. By the time they did, it was May 2003. Cowans had been in jail for nearly six years.

But DNA evidence doesn't spoil easily. Scientists at the lab found evidence on the inside of the baseball hat. They also swabbed the glass for saliva. Both samples produced enough DNA to test. Scientists then created a DNA profile from each sample. They also processed a sample of saliva from Cowans.

Now it was time to compare the finger-prints. Scientists lined up the profiles. The DNA profiles from the cap and the glass were the same. But they did not match Cowans's DNA profile.

To make sure, the court had the white sweatshirt tested. The DNA from it matched the DNA from the cap and glass exactly. But none of the samples matched Cowans's DNA profile.

The lawyers had proved what they suspected all along. Cowans could not have shot Gallagher.

Sergeant Gallagher's attacker left a baseball cap like this one at the scene. Six years later, it was tested for DNA evidence. DNA from the cap did not match Cowans's profile.

Faulty Fingerprint

The print didn't match after all. Cowans walked away a free man.

Cowans had spent six and a half years in jail for a crime he did not commit.

Cowans's lawyer presented the DNA evidence to a judge. The lawyer asked for a new trial. The county **district attorney**, David E. Meier, did not argue. The judge scheduled the trial for January 21, 2004.

In the meantime, Meier got an expert to look again at the fingerprint. This time, the expert said the print did not match Cowans's thumb. Two days later, prosecutors admitted their mistake.

The judge decided there was no need for a new trial. He freed Cowans that day.

On January 23, Stephan Cowans walked out of prison to join his family. "I don't think there are any words in the dictionary to describe what that's like," he said.

The Boston police commissioner publicly apologized to Cowans. "Our error contributed to Mr. Cowans's conviction," he said. "For this we offer him and his family our sincere apology."

The Boston police began investigating the fingerprinting mistake. By 2006, the police still hadn't found a suspect. 24/7

FORENSIC

DOWNLOAD

DNA is in every cell of your body. And information about it is on every page of this section.

IN THIS SECTION:

▶ how James Watson found the SECRET OF LIFE;

▶ why DNA testing is MAKING HEADLINES;

▶ information about the tools FORENSIC SCIENTISTS use to analyze DNA;

▶ whether DNA analysis might be in YOUR FUTURE.

1953 "The Secret of Life"

American scientist James Watson identifies the **double helix**. Watson *(left)* shares a lab in England with Francis Crick *(right)*. The pair know that DNA exists. But no one knows how it works.

One night Watson has a brainstorm. DNA is shaped like a twisted ladder. The rungs are made of chemicals called **bases**. The rails are made of another kind of chemical. Watson walks into a bar and shouts, "We have found the secret of life!"

Key Dates in the

1984 Genetic ID Cards

Sir Alec Jeffreys is the first person to find a way to identify people by their DNA. Jeffreys *(below)* is part of a team studying seal genes when he makes this discovery. He creates a way to take x-rays of DNA. He uses it on human samples. As he develops the film, he sees patterns in the x-rays. He realizes that the patterns change from person to person.

1986 DNA Nabs a Killer

British courts accept DNA as evidence. A 15-year-old is murdered and the killer leaves a trace of blood behind. Police call in Sir Alec Jeffreys to help them catch the killer.

Jeffreys starts the world's first large-scale DNA testing. He takes blood or saliva samples from 5,000 local men. At one point, a man who is not guilty confesses to the crime. But his sample does not match.

The search continues until police find a match, and the killer goes to jail. DNA analysis helps catch a killer. And for the first time it also **exonerates** an innocent man.

1988 DNA Testing Comes to the United States

DNA evidence is used for the first time in a U.S. court. On May 9, 1986, a 27-year-old woman is attacked in her Florida home. Two years later, she identifies Tommy Lee Andrews as her attacker. Andrews tells a jury he was home on May 9. His DNA, however, tells a different story. It matches the DNA from body fluids found at the crime scene. Andrews goes to jail for 115 years.

1990 DNA Database

Virginia becomes the first state to collect DNA from criminals. Police enter the evidence into a computer database.

Study of DNA

How did scientists unlock the secrets of DNA? It didn't happen overnight.

1998 DNA Database Goes National

The FBI sets up its first DNA database. It's called CODIS. The system allows states to work together to link suspects to crimes.

1992 Genes for Justice

The Innocence Project is founded by Barry Scheck (above) and Peter Neufeld. Its goal is to use DNA evidence to free innocent people from jail.

In the News

DNA Tests Could Reunite Families of Holocaust Victims

JERUSALEM, ISRAEL—June 12, 2006

During the Holocaust, thousands of Jewish children lost their parents. Many were also separated from brothers or sisters at a very young age. They have no idea who their parents were. They may have relatives somewhere in the world. But until now, they have had no way of identifying their family members.

Now, according to an American scientist, DNA testing could help bring these families together. Mary-Claire King does genetic research at the University of Washington. She plans to take blood samples from Jews who don't know their roots. She will then also take samples from families who think they have living relatives. Tests could reveal which people come from the same extended families.

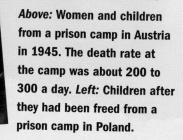

Above: Women and children from a prison camp in Austria in 1945. The death rate at the camp was about 200 to 300 a day. *Left:* Children after they had been freed from a prison camp in Poland.

Scientists get blood samples from a pair of jeans and a T-shirt for a criminal investigation. The scientists will then determine the DNA profile of the blood.

Police Need Help Processing DNA Cases

INDIANAPOLIS, INDIANA—June 13, 2006

Twenty years ago, barely anyone had heard of DNA profiling. Today, police can't get along without it. In fact, some labs can't keep up with the work. These forensic scientists work at the state police lab in Indiana. They have 1,100 DNA cases waiting to be tested. That means many criminal suspects have to wait months for their cases to go to trial.

The state is hiring 20 new scientists. But they still need more help. Police are now sending several hundred cases out to private labs.

A worker in a lab prepares a sample for the thermocycler. That's part of the process of creating a DNA profile.

47

It's All Genetic

Have a look at the tools and equipment used to collect DNA samples—and then to analyze them.

AT THE CRIME SCENE

`swab kit` Police use a swab to collect saliva from the inside of a person's cheek. Then they seal the swab in a paper envelope. This photo shows three swab samples in tubes. The tubes have been placed in a plastic evidence bag.

Tyvek suit Protects investigators from dangerous material. Here, investigators look for clues and evidence at the burial site of a murder victim in England.

MAKING THE SCENE

Here's how to get DNA evidence from a crime scene.

Barry A. J. Fisher is the director of the crime lab for the Los Angeles County Sheriff's Department. He's been investigating crimes for more than 35 years. Getting DNA evidence from a crime scene isn't easy. Here are his tips for doing it right:

1. **Do a walk-through.** See everything before you collect any evidence. Look for how the criminal may have gotten in and out of the area.

2. **Protect the crime scene.** Lots of people work at a crime scene. Photographers, police, medical examiners, sketch artists, firefighters, reporters, you name it. Make sure they don't touch important evidence.

3. **Pick a path.** Choose one path in and out of a crime scene. Make sure everyone uses it. This helps protect any possible evidence.

4. **Record it.** Take pictures of the scene. Videotape it. Sketch it if you have to. And be sure to measure bloodstains.

5. **Collect fragile stuff first.** Fingerprints, footprints, hairs, fibers. These things can get stepped on, blown away, or smudged. It's important to find them and collect them quickly.

6. **No flushing.** Don't use the toilet or turn on faucets. You could be sending important evidence down the drain.

electrophoresis system A machine that separates long strands of DNA from short strands. This helps scientists find the part of the DNA they need to examine.

DNA extraction system This machine extracts DNA from stains, blood, and other fluids. It also turns the DNA into a liquid for further testing.

FMBIO It uses a laser or x-ray to take a picture of the DNA. It produces an image in bar code form.

polymerase chain reaction (PCR) This process allows scientists to duplicate small samples of DNA. It is one of the most important developments in science since the discovery of DNA.

AT THE SCENE AND IN THE LAB

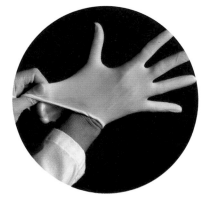

latex gloves Protects the investigator from blood and other samples. Also keeps the investigator from contaminating the evidence.

scalpel A sharp knife to scrape up dried fluids for testing.

DNA: THE INSIDE STORY

What is this stuff, anyway?

When scientists do DNA profiling, they work with the most basic pieces of the body. These pieces are so small you can fit millions of them in the period at the end of this sentence. If you could see them, here's what they would look like.

Chromosomes

Every human has 23 pairs of chromosomes in each cell. Chromosomes contain your genes—about 30,000 of them. Your genes control the way you look and function. You get half your chromosomes from your mother and half from your father. So, you get some of your traits from each of them. You might have your father's black hair and your mother's blue eyes.

DNA

DNA is the chemical that chromosomes and genes are made of. A DNA molecule is shaped like a twisted ladder. The rungs of the ladder hold the information contained in your genes.

WHICH TWIN DID IT?

Identical twins look almost exactly the same. And their DNA is exactly the same, too. So what happens if a twin is a suspect in a crime? DNA evidence can't bail out the innocent one!

There's not the same problem with fraternal twins. They don't look alike, and they don't share the same DNA.

51

HELP WANTED:
DNA Scientist

Is DNA in your genes? Here's more information about the field.

Ann Pollard is a forensic DNA scientist in Virginia.

24/7: How did you decide to become a forensic DNA scientist?

POLLARD: I was always interested in science. I was a biology major, and I learned about forensic science in my classes. I was also interested in law enforcement. This career gives me an opportunity to combine the two: science and law.

24/7: What kind of training did you go through?

POLLARD: I have my bachelor of science degree in biology. I also have a master's degree in criminal justice, with a specialization in forensic science. I took a ten-month training program in forensic biology and DNA analysis.

24/7: What's a typical day like on the job?

POLLARD: When I'm doing case work, I could be working on 15 to 20 cases at a time. I take it one case at a time. I might spend two or three days sitting in the lab. I go through evidence, get samples ready, and stuff like that. Then, I'll spend another week doing actual DNA analysis. Next, I'll write up all the reports and paperwork. That could take about two or three weeks to complete.

24/7: What's the hardest thing for you?

POLLARD: I'd have to say interpreting DNA profiles. We have all these mixtures of samples. And we have to figure out whose DNA it is. People's lives depend on it.

24/7: What's the coolest part about your job?

POLLARD: I get to work on something different all the time. Sometimes, I get basic cases, like finding DNA from a bloodstain or cigarette butt. But every once in a while I get to work on cool stuff, like finding DNA from cans or bottles, guns, hats, clothing, steering wheels—you name it.

THE STATS

MONEY

▶ Forensic scientists may earn $40,000 to $85,000.

▶ Lab directors with advanced degrees can earn more than $100,000.

EDUCATION

▶ B.S. in a hard science, such as biology or biochemistry

▶ M.S. in criminal justice or another hard science

▶ Career training often includes courses in forensic DNA analysis.

THE NUMBERS

▶ There are close to two million DNA samples on file in U.S. state and federal databanks.

▶ As of 2004, in the United States there were 524,700 crime-scene DNA samples waiting to be tested.

▶ Great Britain is the leader in DNA profiles and crime scenes. British investigators make 3,000 DNA matches each month.

24/7: What can middle-school and high-school kids do to get started in the field?

POLLARD: Look for colleges that offer good forensic science programs. It's also important for the school to offer in-depth lab work in the field you want to work in. That way you can get hands-on experience.

Take this totally unscientific quiz to see if you might have what it takes to be a DNA scientist.

1 How do you feel about handling blood?

a) I'm OK with it. I know it can give me valuable information.

b) I'm get a little grossed out. But I can handle it.

c) No, thanks!

2 Can you follow step-by-step directions?

a) That's my strength!

b) Most of the time.

c) I don't like following directions.

3 How organized are you?

a) I'm organized and detailed. I keep notes on everything I do.

b) I'm organized when it comes to homework. But my room is a mess.

c) I can't organize anything. And I'm not good at taking notes.

4 How comfortable are you speaking in public?

a) Bring it on! I love talking to an audience

b) I'm shy. But I can give a speech if I can look at my notes.

c) I wouldn't be caught dead talking to an audience!

5 Can you work independently and also as part of a team?

a) I like working on my own. But I also enjoy working with a team to figure stuff out.

b) I'm best working with a partner or group. But I can sometimes work on my own.

c) I don't like working with a team. I prefer to do it all myself.

YOUR SCORE

Give yourself 3 points for every "**a**" you chose. Give yourself 2 points for every "**b**" you chose. Give yourself 1 point for every "**c**" you chose.

If you got **13–15 points**, you'd probably be a good forensic DNA scientist

If you got **10–12 points**, you might be a good forensic DNA scientist

If you got **5–9 points**, you might want to look at another career!

HOW TO GET STARTED...NOW!

It's never too early to start working toward your goals.

GET AN EDUCATION

▶ Starting now, take as many math and science courses as you can. Train yourself to ask questions, gather evidence, and draw conclusions the way forensic scientists do.

▶ Work on your public speaking skills. Join the debate team, the speech club, or the drama club. It's good practice for testifying in the courtroom.

▶ Start thinking about college. Look for ones that have good science programs. Call or write to those colleges to get information.

▶ Read the newspapers. Keep up with what's happening in your community.

▶ Read anything you can find about DNA analysis. Learn about cases in which DNA played a vital role. See the books and Web sites in the Resources section on pages 56–58.

▶ Graduate from high school!

NETWORK!

Investigate an investigator. Get in touch with your local police department. Interview a crime scene investigator or DNA analyst. Ask to spend a day with him or her to get a sense of what goes on.

GET AN INTERNSHIP

Call your local crime lab. Staff there might be willing to give you a tour. Or there may be internships available. Don't be afraid to ask!

LEARN ABOUT OTHER JOBS IN THE FIELD

There are certain jobs that relate to DNA analysis. They are:
▶ Forensic chemist
▶ Crime scene analyst
▶ Crime scene technician
▶ Criminalist
▶ Crime lab supervisor

Resources

Looking for more information about DNA? Here are some resources you don't want to miss!

PROFESSIONAL ORGANIZATIONS

American Academy of Forensic Sciences (AAFS)
www.aafs.org
410 North 21st Street
Colorado Springs, CO 80904-2798
PHONE: 719-636-1100
FAX: 719-636-1993

The AAFS provides education for people interested in working in forensic science and continuing education for experts already in the field. The organization runs workshops and sessions at its annual meeting that are open for students in middle school and up.

American Society of Crime Laboratory Directors (ASCLD)
www.ascld.org
139K Technology Drive
Garner, NC 27529

The ASCLD is an association of crime laboratory directors and forensic science managers dedicated to providing excellence in forensic science through leadership and innovation.

Canadian Society of Forensic Science (CSFS)
www.csfs.ca
P.O. Box 37040
3332 McCarthy Road
Ottawa, Ontario
Canada K1V 0W0
PHONE: 613-738-0001
EMAIL: csfs@bellnet.ca

The CSFS is open to professionals interested in forensic sciences. The group sends journals to its members four times a year. It also holds meetings, which include forensic workshops.

WEB SITES

Careers in Forensic Science
www.forensicdna.com/careers.htm
An overview of requirements and options for a forensic science career.

Court TV Crime Library
www.crimelibrary.com
Has lots of information about crime and forensics.

Crime Lab Project
www.crimelabproject.com
The Crime Lab Project works to increase awareness of the problems facing public forensic science agencies.

FBI Crime Lab DNA Analysis Unit
www.fbi.gov/hq/lab/org/dnau.htm
For information about the DNA Analysis Unit that analyzes body fluids recovered as evidence in violent crimes.

Forensic Files www.forensic-files.com
Web site for *The Forensic Files* on Court TV, which features real forensic cases.

Interactive Quiz: What Every Law Enforcement Officer Should Know About DNA Evidence
www.dna.gov/training/letraining/beg/menu.htm
Learn about DNA and forensics the way that law enforcement officers do!

BOOKS

Camenson, Blythe. *Opportunities in Forensic Science Careers.* New York: McGraw-Hill, 2001.

Fisher, Barry A. J. *Techniques of Crime Scene Investigation,* 7th ed. Boca Raton, Fla.: CRC Press, 2003.

Genge, Ngaire, E. *The Forensic Casebook: The Science of Crime Scene Investigation.* New York: Ballantine, 2002.

Platt, Richard. *Ultimate Guide to Forensic Science.* New York: DK Publishing, 2003.

Ramsland, Katherine M. *The Forensic Science of CSI.* New York: Berkley Trade, 2001.

Rudin, Norah, and Keith Inman. *An Introduction to Forensic Analysis,* 2nd ed. Boca Raton, Fla.: CRC Press, 2001.

COLLEGES

Only a few schools offer a full-fledged undergraduate degree in forensic science. A greater number allow a minor or concentration in forensic science along with a degree in one of the physical sciences. Here is a selection of colleges to consider, and some of these offer master's degree programs as well:

Albany State University
www.asurams.edu
Forensic Science
Department of Criminal Justice
504 College Drive
Albany, GA 31705
PHONE: 229-430-4864

Buffalo State College
www.buffalostate.edu
Forensic Chemistry
Chemistry Department
313 Science Building
1300 Elmwood Avenue
Buffalo, NY 14222
PHONE: 716-878-5204

George Washington University
www.gwu.edu
Graduate Programs
Department of Forensic Sciences
2036 H Street
Samson Hall
Washington, DC 20052
PHONE: 202-994-7319

John Jay College of Criminal Justice
www.jjay.cuny.edu
Forensic Science
889 Tenth Avenue
New York, NY 10019
PHONE: 212-237-8000

Ohio University
www.ohio.edu
Forensic Chemistry
Athens, OH 45701
PHONE: 740-593-1000

University of Mississippi
www.olemiss.edu
Forensic Chemistry
Department of Chemistry and
  Biochemistry
322 Coulter Hall
University, MS 38677
PHONE: 662-915-7301

Virginia Commonwealth University
www.vcu.edu
Forensic Science
College of Humanities and Sciences
P.O. Box 843079
Richmond, VA 23284
PHONE: 804-828-8420

West Chester University
www.wcupa.edu
Forensic Chemistry
Department of Chemistry
West Chester, PA 19383
PHONE: 610-436-2631

A

alibi (AL-uh-bye) *noun* proof that an accused person was somewhere else when the crime occurred

B

bag (bag) *verb* to take as evidence

bases (bayss-ez) *noun* rungs that make up the DNA ladder

C

chain-of-custody form (chayn ohv KUST-uh-dee form) *noun* a document used to record the names of people who held evidence gathered at a crime scene

chromosomes (KROH-muh-zohmz) *noun* thread-like structures in the center of a cell. They are made of DNA and contain all the genetic information in your body.

CODIS (KOH-diss) *noun* a database that contains DNA samples of more than 300,000 people. It stands for *Combined DNA Index System*.

contamination (kuhn-TAM-uh-nay-shun) *noun* the process that something is made dirty or unfit for use

D

degrade (dee-GRADE) *verb* to break down into small unusable parts

district attorney (DISS-trikt uh-TUR-nee) *noun* a lawyer who represents a certain city or town in criminal trials

DNA (DEE-en-ay) *noun* a chemical found in almost every cell of your body. It's a blueprint for the way you look and function.

DNA profiling (DEE-en-ay PROH-fyl-ing) *noun* a way of processing DNA samples so they can be compared with other samples

double helix (DUH-buhl HEE-lix) *noun* the pair of strands that make up DNA

E

evidence (EHV-uh-denss) *noun* materials, facts, and details collected from a crime scene that offer proof for a crime's conclusion

Dictionary

exonerate (ig-ZAH-nuh-rayte) *verb* to clear a person from blame or guilt

expert (EX-purt) *noun* a person who has a great deal of knowledge and experience in a certain field. See page 12 to learn about forensic experts.

eyewitness (eye-WIT-ness) *noun* a person who saw a crime being committed

F

FBI (EF-bee-eye) *noun* a U.S. government agency that investigates major crimes. It stands for *Federal Bureau of Investigation*.

forensic (fuh-REN-zik) *adjective* describing the science used to investigate and solve crimes

G

genes (jeenz) *noun* tiny pieces of DNA that determine traits in every person

H

hostage (HOSS-tij) *noun* a person who is taken and held prisoner as a way for someone to demand money or other terms

I

isolate (EYE-suh-layt) *verb* to find something; to separate it from everything around it

J

jury (JU-ree) *noun* a group of people at a trial who listen to a court case and decide if a person is guilty or innocent

L

lineup (LYNE-uhp) *noun* a group of people lined up for inspection by police or witnesses

P

perp (purp) *noun* a person who has committed a crime. It's short for *perpetrator*.

polymerase chain reaction (puh-LIM-uh-rase chayn ree-AK-shun) *noun* a process that allows scientists to duplicate small amounts of DNA. Also known as PCR.

prosecutor (PROSS-uh-kyoo-tur) *noun* a lawyer who represents the government in criminal trials

R

RH factor (ahr-aych FAK-tur) *noun* a specific trait that occurs in some red blood cells

S

scalpel (SKAL-puhl) *noun* a small, sharp knife used by surgeons

signature (SIG-nuh-chur) *noun* a characteristic mark

significant (sig-NIF-uh-kuhnt) *adjective* important or having great meaning

specialist (SPE-shuh-list) *noun* someone who has specific knowledge about a given subject

suspect (SUS-pekt) *noun* a person law enforcement officials think might be guilty of a crime

swab (swahb) *verb* to use a thick cotton tip on a stick—like a Q-tip, only bigger—to get samples of DNA

T

trait (trayt) *noun* a specific feature of something or someone

V

verdict (VUR-dikt) *noun* a decision from a jury about whether someone is guilty or innocent

Index

agents, 12
alibis, 30
Andrews, Tommy Lee, 45
animal DNA, 31–32, 34

bagging, 9
barcodes, 22, 48, 50
bases, 44
Beamish, Douglas, 26, 30, 31, 33,
    34, *34*
Bibbins, Gene, 40, *40*
Biohazard Labels, 48
blood, 8, 11, 28, 29, 32, 44, 47,
    49, *49*, 50, 52, 53, 54
blood samples, 46
blood types, 29
Bloodsworth, Kirk, *39*, 40, *40*

chain-of-custody forms, 20
chromosomes, 9, 33, 51, *51*
clothing, 48, 53
CODIS (Combined DNA Index
    System), 24
CODIS (Convicted Offender's DNA
    Identification System), 23,
    24, 45
conclusions, 32, 41, 55
Cowans, Stephen, 36, 37, 38, 39,
    41, 42, *42*
Crick, Francis, 44, *44*
crime scenes, 11, 17, 18, 20, 49,
    49, 52, 54

degradation, 9
detectives, 11, 12, 30, 31, 32
district attorneys, 42
DNA (Deoxyribonucleic Acid), 8, 10,
    11, 12, 33, 44, 49-54, *51*
DNA barcodes, 22, 48, 49

DNA evidence, 20, 39, 40, 41, 42,
    44, 45, 49
DNA extraction systems, 49, 50, *50*
DNA molecules, 33, 51, *51*
DNA profiling, 8, 22, 23, 33, 41, 47,
    51, 53
Duguay, Shirley, 26, *26*, 28–29,
    30, 33

education, 52, 53, 54, 55
electrophoresis system, 50, *50*
evidence, 9, 11, 12, 14, 17, 18,
    19, 20, 21, 30, 31, 32, 34,
    37, 39, 40, 41, 42, 44, 45,
    48, 49, 50, 52, 54
evidence envelopes, 48
eyewitnesses, 40–41

face masks, *49*
Feldman, Robert N., 38, 39
fingerprint specialists, 12
fingerprints, 12, 21, 37, 38, 39,
    41, 49
Fisher, Barry A. J., 18, 49, *49*
FMBIO machines, 22, 49, 50, *50*
forensic scientists, 12, 14, 39, 47,
    49, 50, 52, *52*, 54
fraternal twins, 51, *51*

Gallagher, Gregory, 36, 37
genes, 9, 33, 50, *50*, 52
gloves, 19, 20, 48, *49*, 50, *50*
goggles, 50

Holocaust, 46
hostages, 37

identical twins, 8, 51, *51*
Innocence Project, 38, 40, 45
isolation, 21

Jeffreys, Sir Alec, 44, *44*
Jones, Joan, 19–20, *19*
juries, 31, 33, 34, 36, 37

King, Mary-Claire, 46

lab coats, 50, *50*
latex gloves, 19, 20, 48, *49*, 50, *50*
Leahy, Sen. Patrick, *39*
lineups, 37, 38

MacNeil, Alphonse, 30, 34
medical examiners, 12, 49, *49*
Meier, David E., 42
molecules, 33
Moon, Brandon, 40, *40*

Neufeld, Peter, *38*, 40, 45

O'Brien, Stephen, 32, 34

perps, 9, 24
Pollard, Ann, 21–22, *21*, 23, 52–53, *52*
polymerase chain reaction (PCR), 22, 50
prosecutors, 31, 34, 36

quiz, 54

RH factor, 29

saliva samples, 21, 41, 44
Savoie, Roger, 31, 32
scalpels, 21, 50, *50*
Scheck, Barry, *38*, 40, 45, *45*
Shepard, David, 40, *40*
Snowball (cat), 31–32, 34
specimen collection swab kits, 48
swabbing, 9, 21, 23, 41, 48

thermocyclers, 22
tools, 50–51, *50*
trace evidence specialists, 12
traits, 8, 51
twins, 8, 51, *51*
TYVEK suits, 48

verdicts, 34

walk-through, 18, 49
Watson, James, 44, *44*

Author's Note

After more than 250 pages of research about DNA and crime, I became intrigued with every case—especially unsolved cases. I'd search the Internet for clues to the case, hoping to find information that would help solve a crime.

But as the book's deadline approached, I snapped back to reality. I'm not a DNA analyst or crime scene investigator. I'm an author! My job is to *write* about crimes, not solve them.

If you're interested in a career in forensic science, start with your own neighborhood. Dial the number of the county medical examiner's office. When you call the ME office, explain who you are and what you need. Say something like, "Hi, my name is (fill in the blank!). I'm a student at (fill in the blank with your school name and town). I'm seriously considering a career in forensic science. I was wondering if there's a (choose one) DNA scientist, blood spatter specialist, forensic anthropologist, or fingerprint specialist who could take a few minutes to talk to me?"

You'll likely be connected to someone who can help. Talk to the person about his or her job. Ask what a typical day is like. Most people chose a career in forensic science because it's an opportunity to help society. So they'll be more than happy to help you— just be aware that they may be time-crunched because they're working on a case!

ACKNOWLEDGMENTS

Many thanks to the following people for their expertise: Jan Burke, Barry A. J. Fisher, David Vidal, Joan Jones, and Ann Pollard.

CONTENT ADVISER: Norah Rudin, PhD, Forensic DNA Consultant